FINGERPICKING BLUES

Arrangements by Chad Johnson

ISBN 978-1-4234-8743-2

HAL•LEONARD®
CORPORATION

7777 W. BLUEMOUND RD. P.O. BOX 13819 MILWAUKEE, WI 53213

Visit Hal Leonard Online at
www.halleonard.com

CONTENTS

Baby Please Don't Go

Words and Music by Joseph Lee Williams

1. Ba - by, please don't go. _____

3. See additional lyrics

Ba - by, please don't go. _____   Ba - by, please don't go. _____

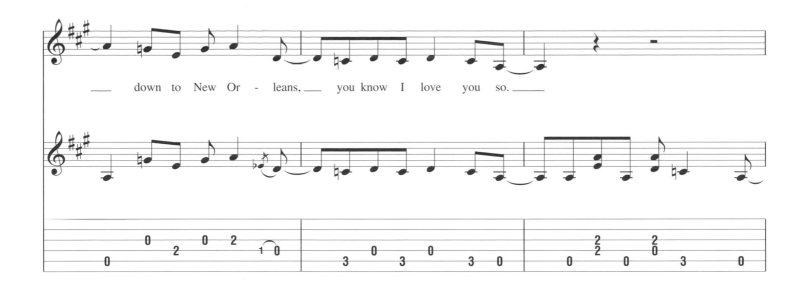

down to New Or - leans, ___ you know I love you so. ___

Verse
A

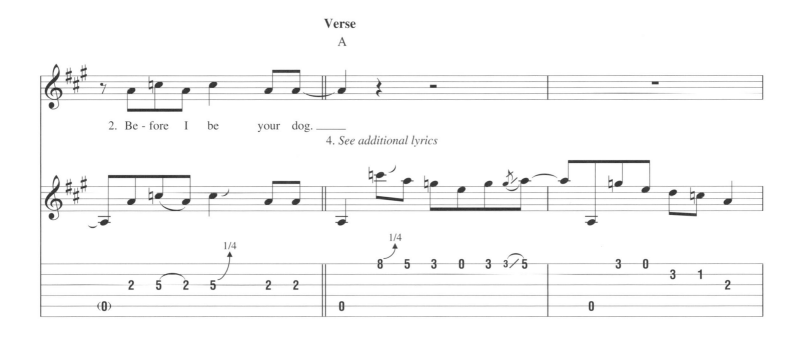

2. Be - fore I be your dog. ___

4. See additional lyrics

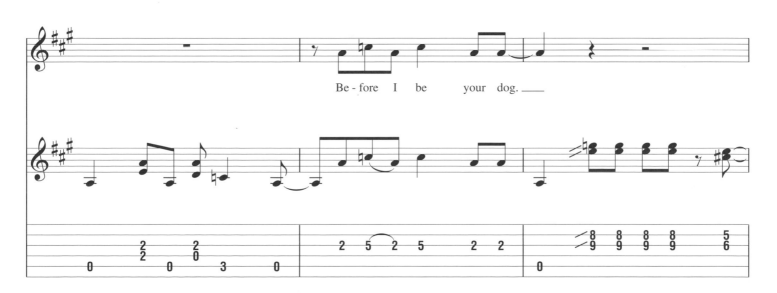

Be - fore I be your dog. ___

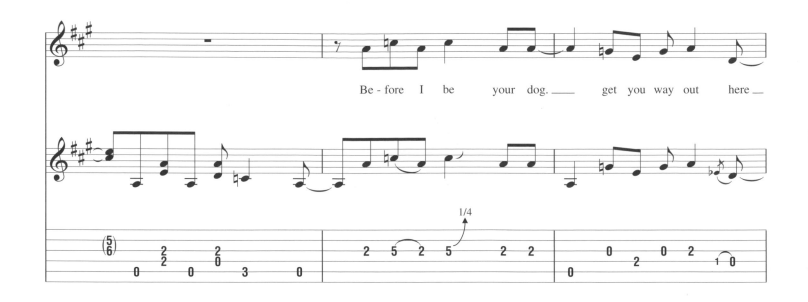

Be - fore I be your dog.___ get you way out here___

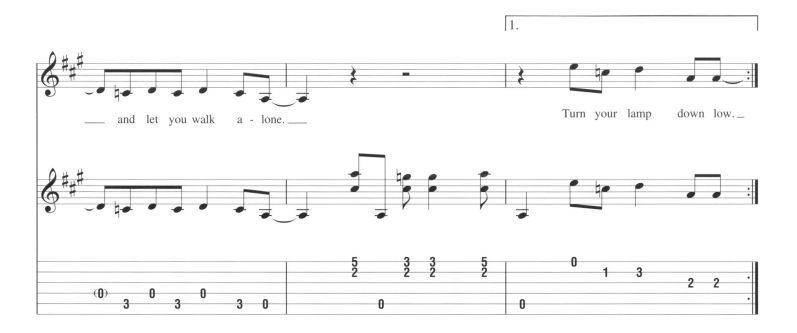

1.

___ and let you walk a - lone.___

Turn your lamp down low.___

2.

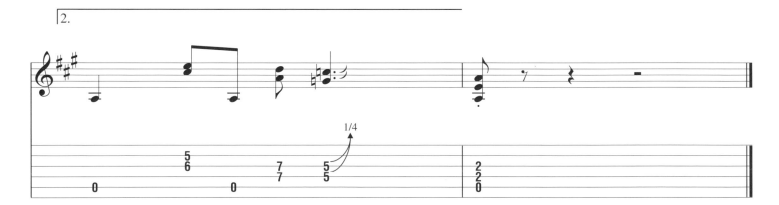

Additional Lyrics

3. Turn your lamp down low.
   Turn your lamp down low.
   Turn your lamp down low.
   I'll beg you all night long, baby, please don't go,

4. You know your man done gone,
   You know your man done gone.
   You know your man done gone
   Down the county farm, he's got his shackles on.

Come On in My Kitchen

Words and Music by Robert Johnson

Drop D tuning:
(low to high) D-A-D-G-B-E

Intro
Moderately

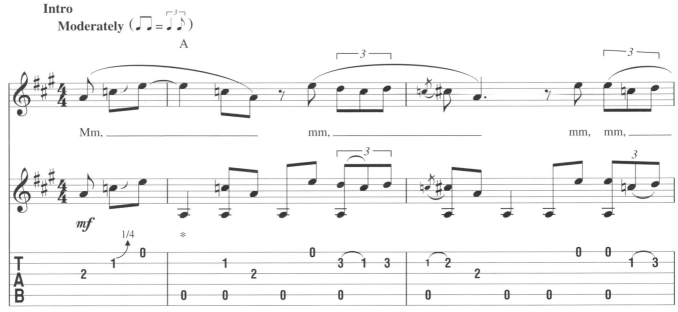

*Slight palm mute on 5th and 6th strings throughout.

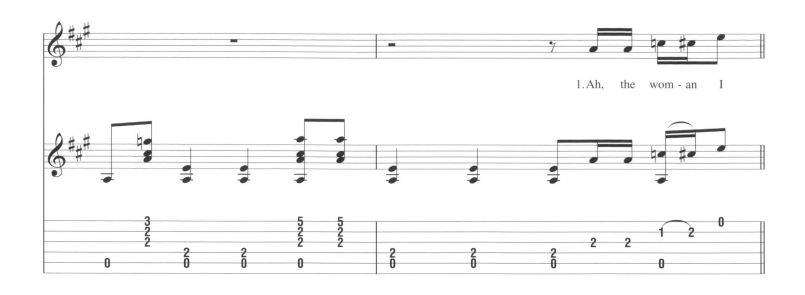

1. Ah, the wom - an I

§ Verse

love   took from my best friend.   Some jok - er got luck - y, stole her back a -

2., 3., 4. See additional lyrics

gain.   You bet - ter come on   in my kitch - en.   Babe, it's

Additional Lyrics

2. Ah, she's gone. I know she won't come back.
   I've taken the last nickel out of her nation sack.
   You better come on in my kitchen.
   Babe, it's goin' to be rainin' outdoors.

3. When a woman gets in trouble, ev'rybody throws her down.
   Lookin' for her good friend, none can be found.
   You better come on in my kitchen.
   Babe, it's goin' to be rainin' outdoors.

4. Winter time's comin', it's gon' be slow.
   You can't make the winter, babe, that's dry long so.
   You better come on in my kitchen,
   'Cause it's goin' to be rainin' outdoors.

Bright Lights, Big City

Words and Music by Jimmy Reed

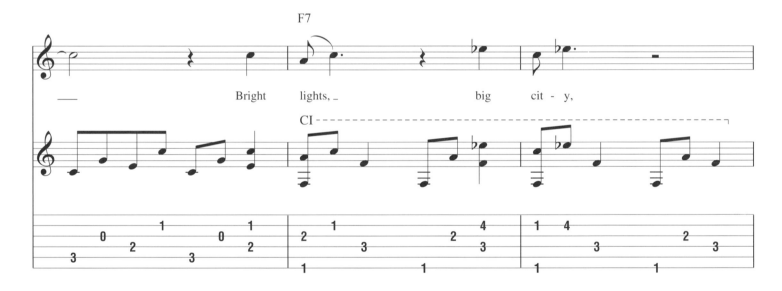

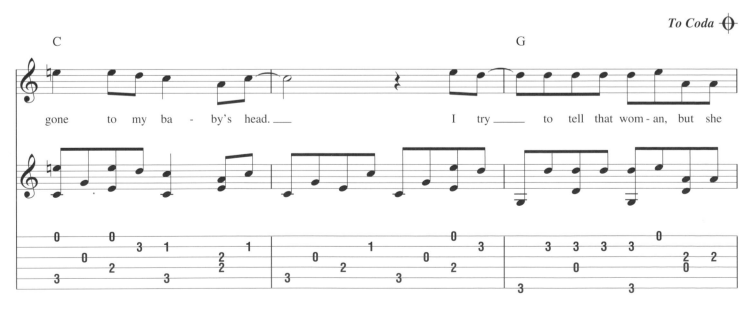

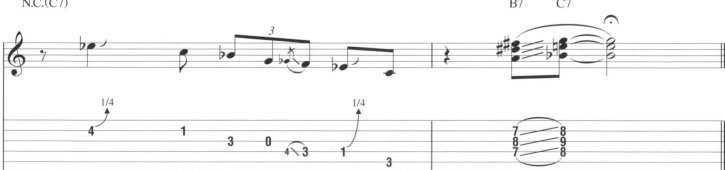

Additional Lyrics

2. It's all right, pretty baby, gonna need my help someday.
   It's all right, pretty baby, gonna need my help someday.
   You gonna wish you had a-listened to some of those things I said.

3. Go ahead, pretty baby, honey knock yourself out.
   Go ahead, pretty baby, honey knock yourself out.
   I still love ya, baby, 'cause you don't know what it's all about.

Darlin' You Know I Love You

Words and Music by B.B. King and Jules Bihari

morn - ing.   I   dream   of you   ev - 'ry   night _____   and would

love,   love __ to   be   with you   al - ways.

Bridge

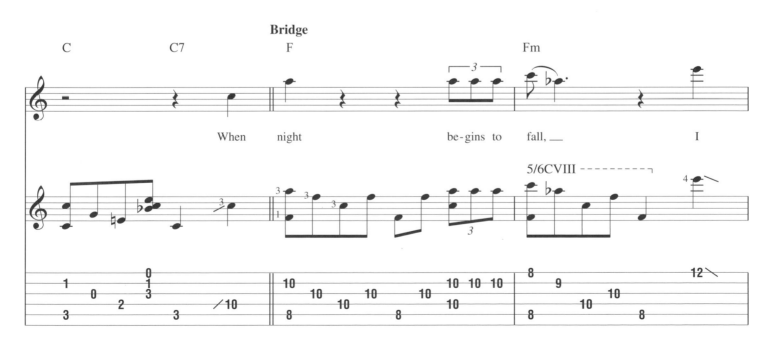

When   night   be - gins to   fall, __   I

cry, _____ cry a - lone.   And I wish   I could

D.C. al Coda

hold you   in my arms   to - night.   3. Oh, oh, ___

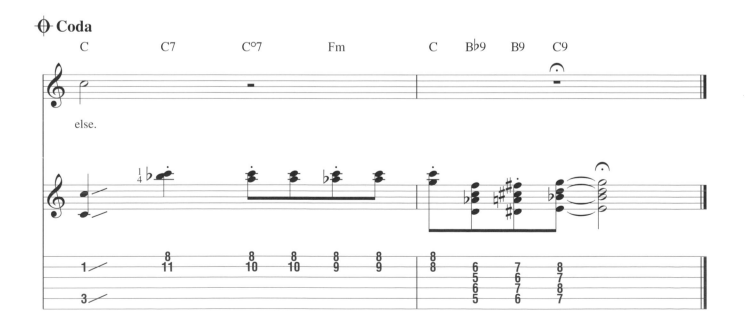

else.

How Long, How Long Blues

Words and Music by Leroy Carr

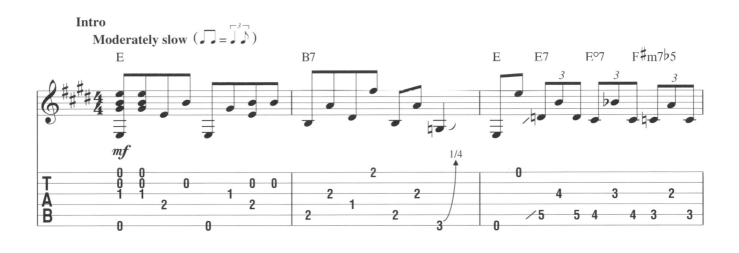

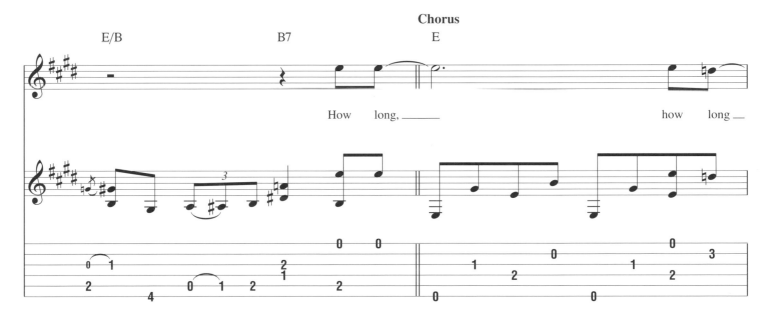

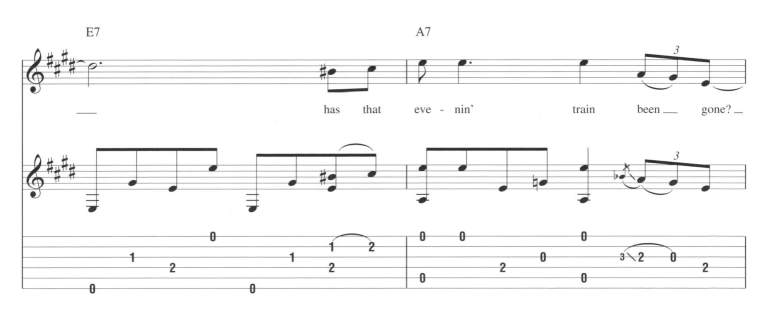

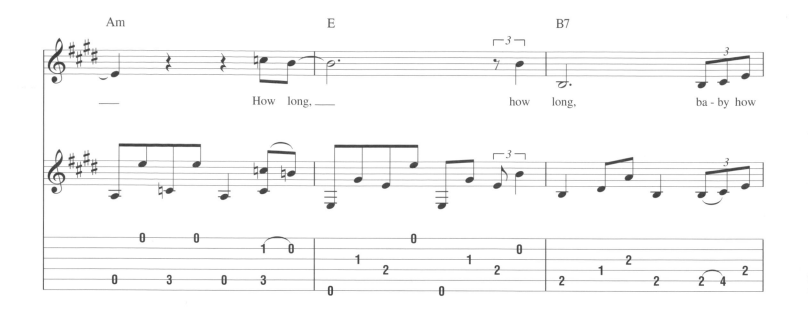

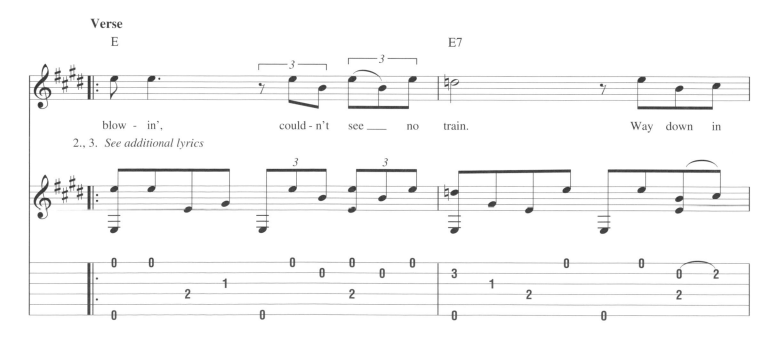

my ___ heart ___ I had an ach - in' pain. ___   How long, ___

___   how long,   ba - by how long?

2. Some - times   I
3. And   if   I could

Additional Lyrics

2. Sometimes I feel so disgusted, and I feel so blue
   That I hardly know what in this world, baby, just to do.
   But how long, how, how long, baby, how long?

3. And if I could holler, like I was a mountain jack,
   I'd go up on the mountain, I'd call my baby back.
   But how long, how, how long, baby, how long?

Everyday I Have the Blues

Words and Music by Peter Chatman

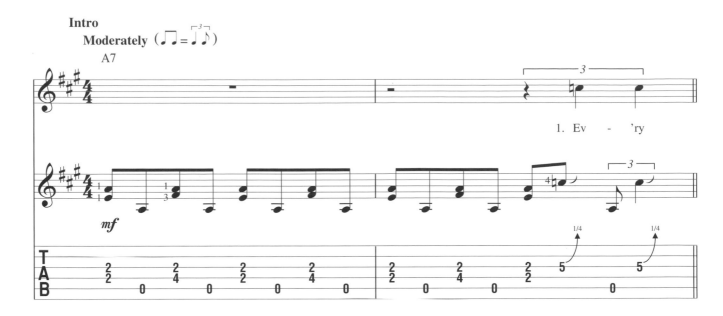

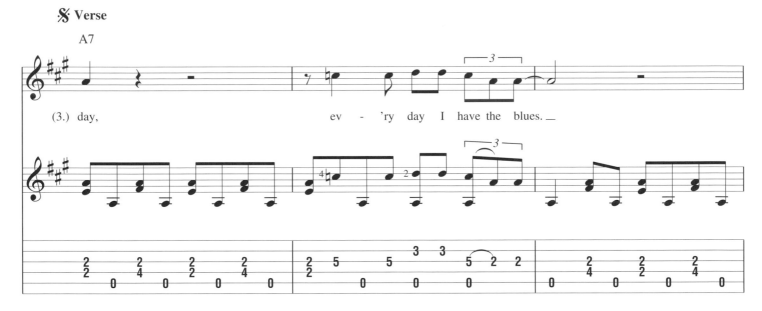

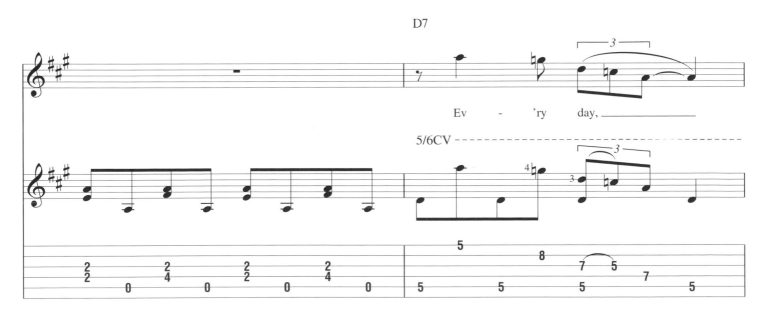

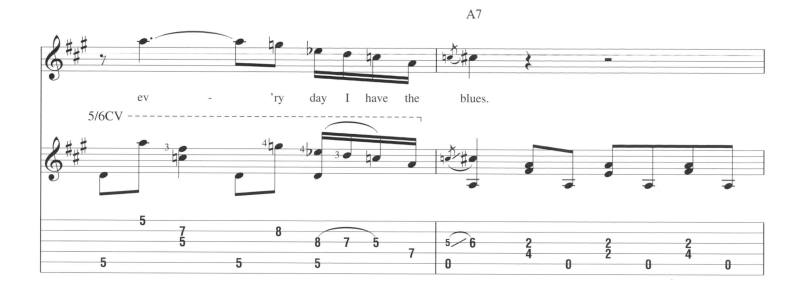

ev - 'ry day I have the blues.

When you see me wor - ry babe,

yeah, _____ it's you _ I hate to lose.　2., 4. Well, _____

Verse

no - bod - y loves me, no - bod - y seems to care.

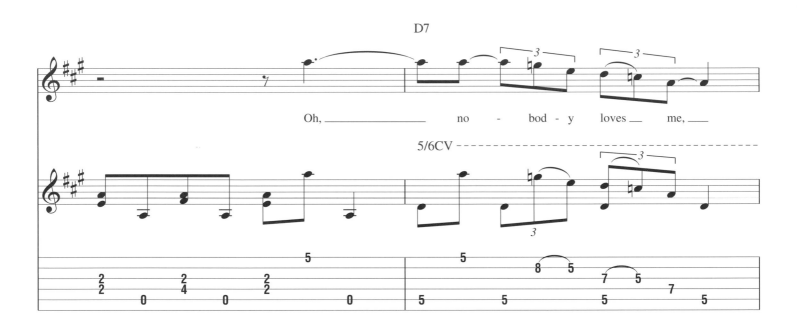

Oh, _____ no - bod - y loves _____ me, _____

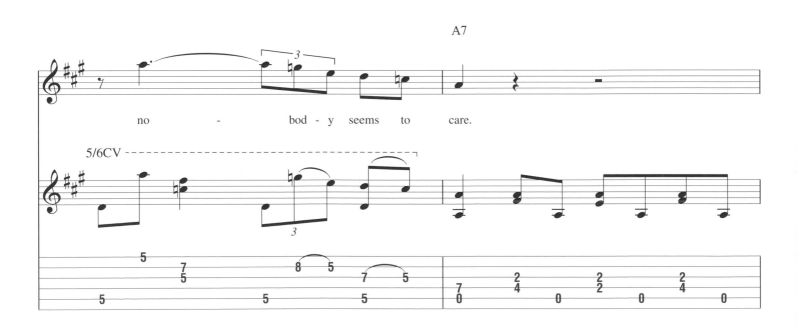

no - bod - y seems to care.

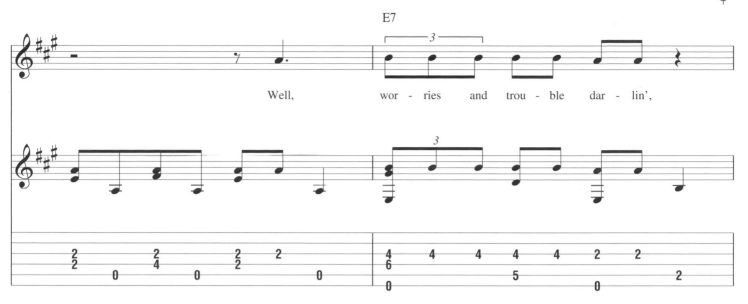

Well, wor - ries and trou - ble dar - lin',

D.S. al Coda

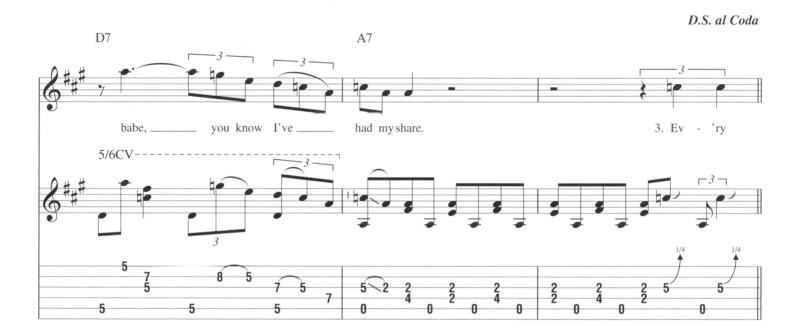

babe, _____ you know I've _____ had my share. 3. Ev - 'ry

⊕ **Coda**

babe, you know _ I've had my share.

Further On Up the Road

Words and Music by Joe Veasey and Don Robey

1. Fur-ther on up the road, ___ some-one's gon-na hurt you like

2.- 4. *See additional lyrics*

you hurt me. ___ Fur-ther on ___ up the road, ___

some-one's gon-na hurt you like you hurt me. ___ Fur-ther on _____ up the

Additional Lyrics

2. You got to reap just what you sow. That ol' saying is true.
   You got to reap just what you sow. That ol' saying is true.
   Like you mistreat someone, someone's gonna mistreat you.

3. Now you're laughin', pretty baby. Someday you gonna be cryin'.
   Now you're laughin', pretty baby. Someday you gonna be cryin'.
   Further on up the road, you'll find out I wasn't lyin'.

4. Further on up the road, when you're alone 'n' blue,
   Further on up the road, when you're alone 'n' blue,
   You gonna ask me to take you back, baby, but I'll have somebody new.

I Ain't Superstitious

Written by Willie Dixon

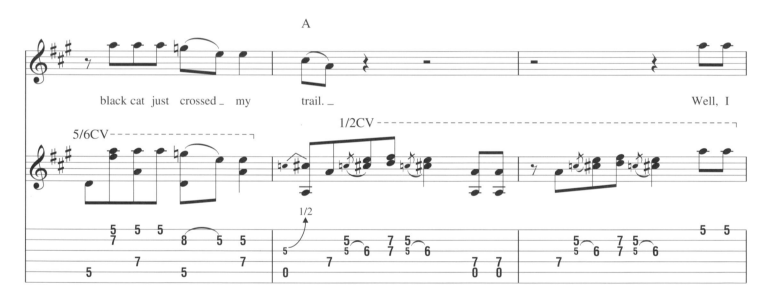

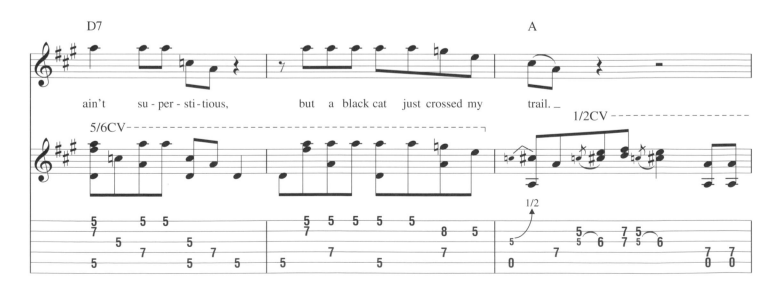

Additional Lyrics

2. When my right hand is itchin', I get money for sure.
   When my right hand is itchin', I get money for sure.
   But when my left starts jumpin', somebody's got to go.

3. Well, the dogs all howlin', all over the neighborhood.
   Well, the dogs all howlin', all over the neighborhood.
   That is a true sign of death, baby, that ain't no good.

It Hurts Me Too

Words and Music by Mel London

Drop D tuning:
(low to high) D-A-D-G-B-E

Intro

Slowly

1. You said you was

% Verse

hurt - ing,   you al-most lost your mind.   Now the man you

2., 3., 4. *See additional lyrics*

love, _____   he hurt you all the time.   But when things go ___

Additional Lyrics

2. You love him more when you should love him less.
   Why pick up behind him, and take his mess?
   But when things go wrong, go wrong with you,
   It hurts me too.

3. He love another woman. Yes, I love you.
   But you love him, and stick to him like glue.
   But when things go wrong, go wrong with you,
   It hurts me too.

4. Now, he better leave you or you better put him down.
   No, I won't stand to see you pushed around.
   But when things go wrong, go wrong with you,
   It hurts me too.

Key to the Highway

Words and Music by Big Bill Broonzy and Chas. Segar

Additional Lyrics

2. I'm goin' back to the border
   Where I'm better known.
   Though you haven't done nothin',
   Drove a good man away from home.

3. Oh, gimme one more kiss, mama,
   Just before I go,
   'Cause when I leave this time,
   I won't be back no more.

My Babe

Written by Willie Dixon

Additional Lyrics

2. My babe, I know she loves me, my babe.
Whoa yes, I know she loves me, my baby.
Oh yes, I know she loves me.
She don't do nothing but kiss and hug me.
My babe, true little baby, my babe.

3. My baby don't stand no cheatin', my babe.
Oh no, she don't stand no cheatin', my baby.
Oh no, she don't stand no cheatin'.
Ev'rything she do, she do so pleasin'.
My babe, true little baby, my babe.

4. My baby don't stand no foolin', my babe.
Oh yeah, she don't stand no foolin', my baby.
Oh yeah, she don't stand no foolin'.
When she's hot there ain't no coolin'.
My babe, true little baby, my babe.

Nobody Knows You When You're Down and Out

Words and Music by Jimmie Cox

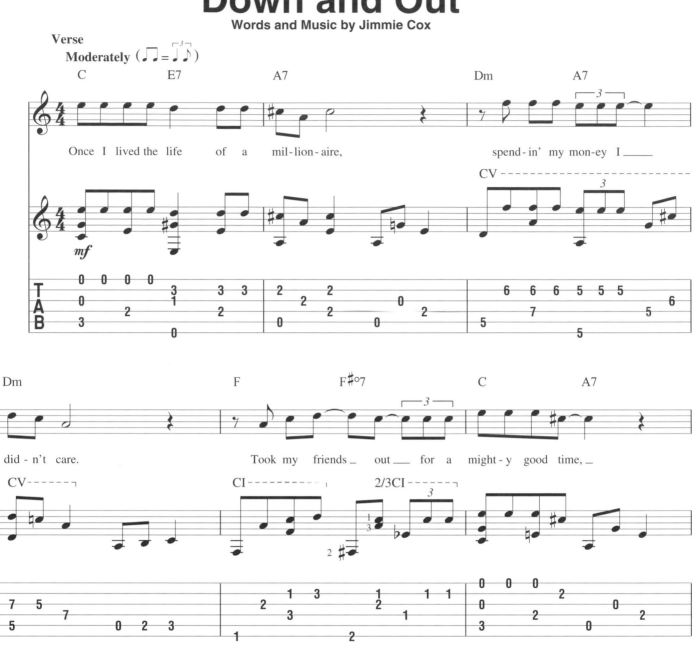

so low, lost all my friends, had no place to go. If I get my hands on a

dol-lar a-gain, I'm gon-na squeeze it 'til the ea - gle grins.

𝄋 Chorus

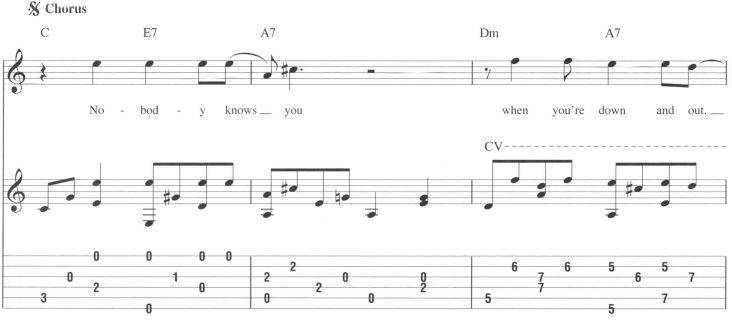

No - bod - y knows you when you're down and out.

To Coda ⊕

Reconsider Baby

Words and Music by Lowell Fulson

oh, how I hate __ to see you go. ___ And the

way that I will miss you, I guess you will __ nev-er know. __

%. **Verse**

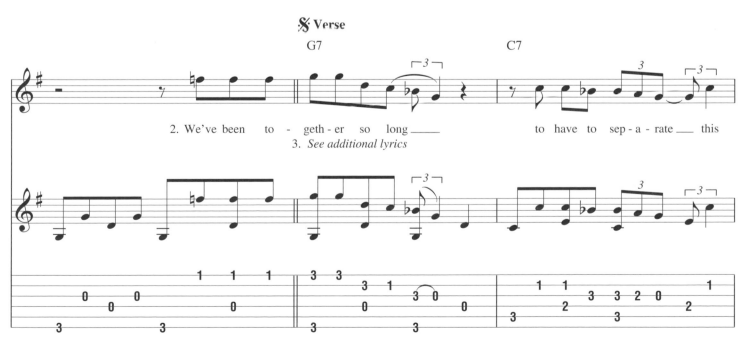

2. We've been to - geth-er so long _____ to have to sep-a-rate __ this
3. *See additional lyrics*

G7

way. We've been to - geth - er so long_____

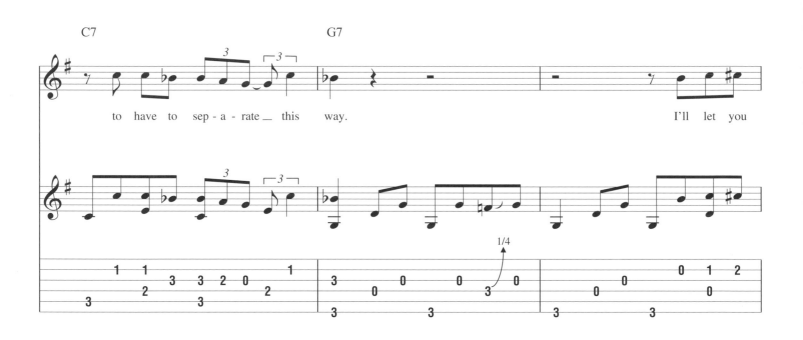

C7   G7

to have to sep - a - rate ___ this way.   I'll let you

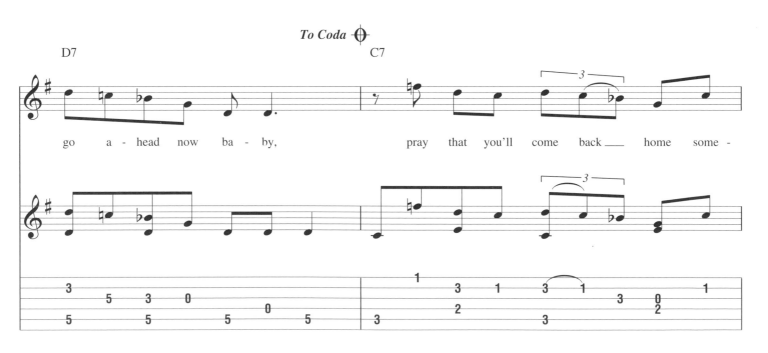

To Coda ⊕

D7   C7

go a - head now ba - by,   pray that you'll come back ___ home some -

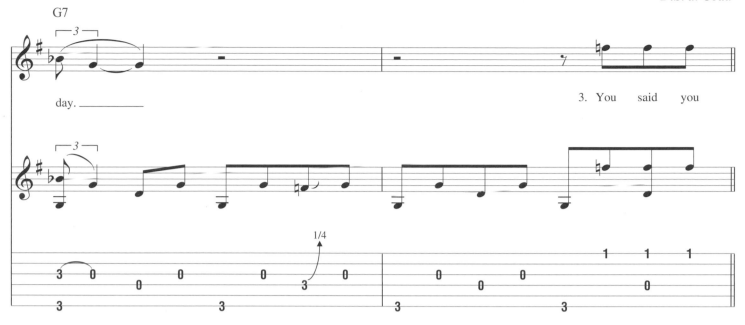

Additional Lyrics

3. You said you once had loved me, but now I guess you have changed your mind.
   You said you once had loved me, but now I guess you have changed your mind.
   Why don't you reconsider, baby, give yourself just a little more time.

(They Call It) Stormy Monday

(Stormy Monday Blues)

Words and Music by Aaron "T-Bone" Walker

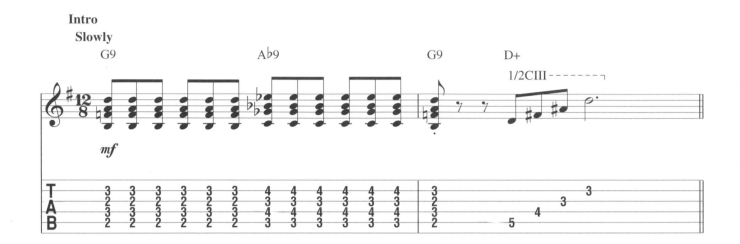

1. They call it storm-y Mon-day, ___ but Tues-day's just as bad. ___
2., 3. *See additional lyrics*

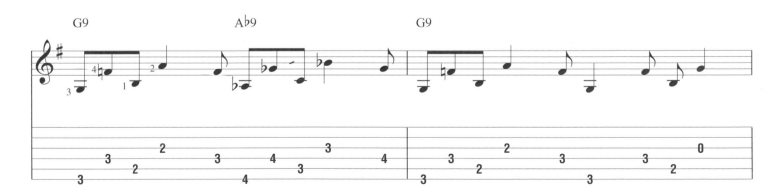

They call it storm-y Mon-day, _____ but Tues-day's just as bad. __

To Coda ⊕

Wednes-day's worse and Thurs-day's al - so

Coda

Additional Lyrics

2. Yeah, the eagle flies on Friday, and Saturday I go out to play.
   The eagle flies on Friday, and Saturday I go out to play.
   Sunday I go to church, and I kneel down and pray.

3. Lord have mercy, Lord have mercy on me.
   Lord have mercy, my heart's in misery.
   Crazy 'bout my baby, please, send her home back to me.

Three Hours Past Midnight

Words and Music by Johnny Watson and Saul Bihari

three hours ___ past mid - night, and my ___ ba - by's ___ no-

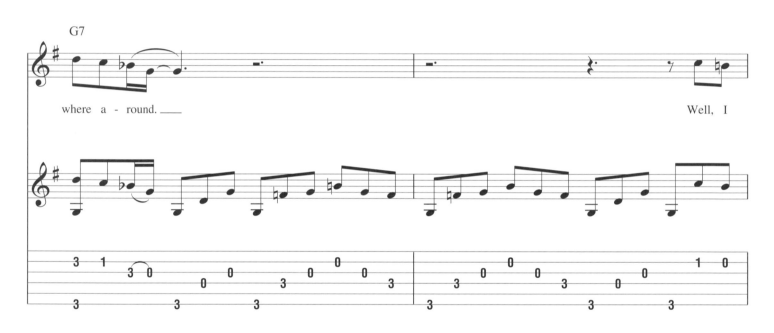

where a - round. ___ Well, I

To Coda ⊕

lis - ten so hard to hear her foot - steps, and I ain't e - ven ___ heard a

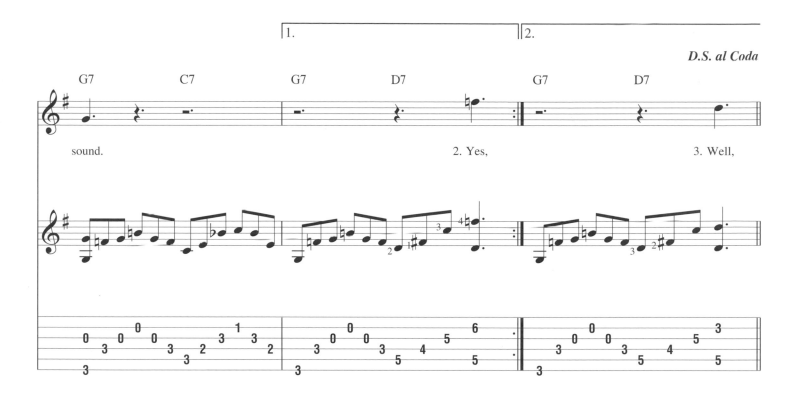

D.S. al Coda

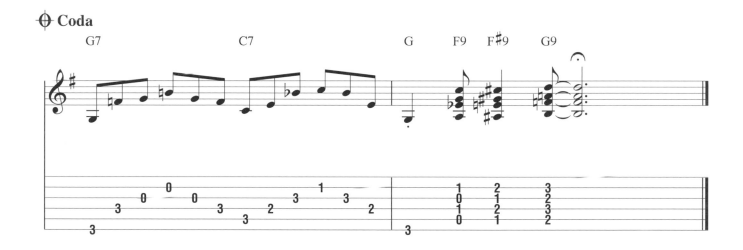

Additional Lyrics

2. Yes, I tossed and tumbled on my pillow, but I just can't close my eyes.
   Yes, I tossed and tumbled on my pillow, but I just can't close my eyes.
   If my baby don't come back pretty quick,
   Yes, I just can't be satisfied.

3. Well, I want my baby, I want her by my side.
   Well, I want my baby, yes, I want her by my side.
   Well, and if she don't come home pretty soon,
   Yes, I just can't be satisfied.

INTRODUCTION TO FINGERSTYLE GUITAR

Fingerstyle (a.k.a. fingerpicking) is a guitar technique that means you literally pick the strings with your right-hand fingers and thumb. This contrasts with the conventional technique of strumming and playing single notes with a pick (a.k.a. flatpicking). For fingerpicking, you can use any type of guitar: acoustic steel-string, nylon-string classical, or electric.

THE RIGHT HAND

The most common right-hand position is shown here.

Use a high wrist; arch your palm as if you were holding a ping-pong ball. Keep the thumb outside and away from the fingers, and let the fingers do the work rather than lifting your whole hand.

The thumb generally plucks the bottom strings with downstrokes on the left side of the thumb and thumbnail. The other fingers pluck the higher strings using upstrokes with the fleshy tip of the fingers and fingernails. The thumb and fingers should pluck one string per stroke and not brush over several strings.

Another picking option you may choose to use is called hybrid picking (a.k.a. plectrum-style fingerpicking). Here, the pick is usually held between the thumb and first finger, and the three remaining fingers are assigned to pluck the higher strings.

THE LEFT HAND

The left-hand fingers are numbered 1 through 4.

Be sure to keep your fingers arched, with each joint bent; if they flatten out across the strings, they will deaden the sound when you fingerpick. As a general rule, let the strings ring as long as possible when playing fingerstyle.

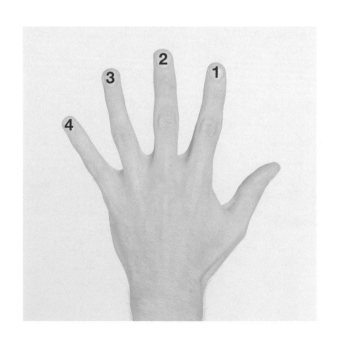

FINGERPICKING GUITAR BOOKS

Hone your fingerpicking skills with these great songbooks featuring solo guitar arrangements in standard notation and tablature. The arrangements in these books are carefully written for intermediate-level guitarists. Each song combines melody and harmony in one superb guitar fingerpicking arrangement. Each book also includes an introduction to basic fingerstyle guitar.

    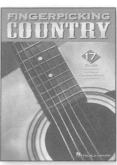 

Fingerpicking Acoustic
00699614 15 songs.....................$14.99

Fingerpicking Acoustic Classics
00160211 15 songs.....................$16.99

Fingerpicking Acoustic Hits
00160202 15 songs.....................$12.99

Fingerpicking Acoustic Rock
00699764 14 songs.....................$14.99

Fingerpicking Ballads
00699717 15 songs.....................$14.99

Fingerpicking Beatles
00699049 30 songs.....................$24.99

Fingerpicking Beethoven
00702390 15 pieces.....................$10.99

Fingerpicking Blues
00701277 15 songs.....................$10.99

**Fingerpicking
Broadway Favorites**
00699843 15 songs.....................$9.99

Fingerpicking Broadway Hits
00699838 15 songs.....................$7.99

Fingerpicking Campfire
00275964 15 songs.....................$12.99

Fingerpicking Celtic Folk
00701148 15 songs.....................$10.99

Fingerpicking Children's Songs
00699712 15 songs.....................$9.99

Fingerpicking Christian
00701076 15 songs.....................$12.99

Fingerpicking Christmas
00699599 20 carols.....................$10.99

**Fingerpicking
Christmas Classics**
00701695 15 songs.....................$7.99

Fingerpicking Christmas Songs
00171333 15 songs.....................$10.99

Fingerpicking Classical
00699620 15 pieces.....................$10.99

Fingerpicking Country
00699687 17 songs.....................$12.99

Fingerpicking Disney
00699711 15 songs.....................$16.99

**Fingerpicking
Early Jazz Standards**
00276565 15 songs.....................$12.99

Fingerpicking Duke Ellington
00699845 15 songs.....................$9.99

Fingerpicking Enya
00701161 15 songs.....................$16.99

Fingerpicking Film Score Music
00160143 15 songs.....................$12.99

Fingerpicking Gospel
00701059 15 songs.....................$9.99

Fingerpicking Hit Songs
00160195 15 songs.....................$12.99

Fingerpicking Hymns
00699688 15 hymns.....................$12.99

Fingerpicking Irish Songs
00701965 15 songs.....................$10.99

Fingerpicking Italian Songs
00159778 15 songs.....................$12.99

Fingerpicking Jazz Favorites
00699844 15 songs.....................$12.99

Fingerpicking Jazz Standards
00699840 15 songs.....................$10.99

Fingerpicking Elton John
00237495 15 songs.....................$14.99

Fingerpicking Latin Favorites
00699842 15 songs.....................$12.99

Fingerpicking Latin Standards
00699837 15 songs.....................$15.99

**Fingerpicking
Andrew Lloyd Webber**
00699839 14 songs.....................$16.99

Fingerpicking Love Songs
00699841 15 songs.....................$14.99

Fingerpicking Love Standards
00699836 15 songs.....................$9.99

Fingerpicking Lullabyes
00701276 16 songs.....................$9.99

Fingerpicking Movie Music
00699919 15 songs.....................$14.99

Fingerpicking Mozart
00699794 15 pieces.....................$9.99

Fingerpicking Pop
00699615 15 songs.....................$14.99

Fingerpicking Popular Hits
00139079 14 songs.....................$12.99

Fingerpicking Praise
00699714 15 songs.....................$14.99

Fingerpicking Rock
00699716 15 songs.....................$14.99

Fingerpicking Standards
00699613 17 songs.....................$14.99

Fingerpicking Wedding
00699637 15 songs.....................$10.99

Fingerpicking Worship
00700554 15 songs.....................$14.99

**Fingerpicking Neil Young –
Greatest Hits**
00700134 16 songs.....................$16.99

Fingerpicking Yuletide
00699654 16 songs.....................$12.99

Prices, contents and availability subject to change without notice.